Puzzling Poems to drive you Crazy

Stornoway Primary School
James Street Drive
Stornoway
Isle of Lewis
HS1 2LF
Tel: 01851 703418/703621
Fax: 01851 706257
E Mail: stornoway-primary@cne-siar.gov.uk

Look out for other books by Susie Gibbs:

Scary Poems to Make You Shiver
Funny Poems to Give You the Giggles
Revolting Poems to Make You Squirm

Poems for My Best Friend

Puzzling Poems to drive you Crazy

Collected by Susie Gibbs
Illustrated by Kelly Waldek

Hee-hee!

OXFORD
UNIVERSITY PRESS

OXFORD
UNIVERSITY PRESS

Great Clarendon Street, Oxford OX2 6DP

Oxford University Press is a department of the University of Oxford.
It furthers the University's objective of excellence in research, scholarship,
and education by publishing worldwide in

Oxford   New York

Auckland   Cape Town   Dar es Salaam   Hong Kong   Karachi
Kuala Lumpur   Madrid   Melbourne   Mexico City   Nairobi
New Delhi   Shanghai   Taipei   Toronto

With offices in

Argentina   Austria   Brazil   Chile   Czech Republic   France   Greece
Guatemala   Hungary   Italy   Japan   Poland   Portugal   Singapore
South Korea   Switzerland   Thailand   Turkey   Ukraine   Vietnam

Oxford is a registered trade mark of Oxford University Press
in the UK and in certain other countries

British Library Cataloguing in Publication Data
Data available

ISBN 978-0-19-272608-7

5 7 9 10 8 6 4

Printed in Great Britain by Cox & Wyman,
Reading, Berkshire

Paper used in the production of this book is a natural,
recyclable product made from wood grown in sustainable forests.
The manufacturing process conforms to the environmental
regulations of the country of origin.

Contents

Peggy Babcock

Peggy Babcock was her name—
Quite ordinary, but problems came
When, amid much giggling, sir
Called the morning register:

Pebby Bagpock . . . I mean
Pecky Bobcack
Boggy Peckback
Packy Backpock
Pabby Begback
Baggy Pepcock
Pocky Bogpack
Poggy Beckback
Becky Popcock . . . er . . .

Think you can do better?
OK, have a blast:
Peggy Babcock ten times—
Fast!

Eric Finney

Found it Yet?

You'll find it
    in a four-leaf clover
    or
    in the heart of your beloved
    or
    at the end of your glove
    or
    all over

You'll find it
    if you look for it

James Carter

Huh?

Eh?

IT ('s a) Riddle

Log on with no danger of burning,
My mouse eats no cheese,
My web has no spiders,
My net catches no fish,
Surf without sea
If you recognize me.

Daphne Kitching

Have you worked it out?

Growing Up in Rome

At the age of four I answered to Ivy.
At six my name was Vi.
At 40 I felt I could really excel
At anything I'd try.

At 54 you could call me Liv,
But I knew I was getting old,
When, at 99, I had a dreadful feeling
Of being really cold.

Rob Falconer

Fighting Men

These brave-hearted men would bring many a cheer
Can you find who they were by the clues hidden here?

Their first is in **fighting** and there appears twice
Their second's in **glory** which carried a price
Their third is in **armour** which some of them wore
Whilst their fourth is in **dagger** and also in **sword**
Their fifth is in **trident** and also in **chain**
Their sixth is in **anguish** as well as in **pain**
Their seventh's in **terror** which all of them knew
And their eighth is in **freedom** which was won
  by a few
Their ninth's in **arena** where many would fall
Whilst their last is in **Spartacus**, greatest of all.

Richard Caley

Four Sports

serve an

4 return

volley

Just it over the

bɛk the

To a ᵏg

A well-placed er

Can please the

 off the "🌀" board

And land in the ⌂

Small kids do "🐕" 🥄.

👁 prefer the "👶"

The ᴺᵇ 🧱 's an odd ▲●◼

We group in a ⱷ sc 🥁

👁 S 🧪 a try

Then convert and we've 𝟙

Beverley Johnson

That Dreadful Pupil from Leicester

There was a young pupil from Leicester
Who would go to her teachers and peicester
She would lock them indoors
Glue their feet to the floors
Till finally they came to arreicester

Trevor Millum

-Snigger!

Ummm....?

Ounce Poem

Mmmm...

A girl who weighed many an oz,
Used language I dare not pronoz,
   For a fellow unkind
   Pulled her chair out behind
Just to see (so he said) if she'd boz.

Anon.

She Called Him Mr

She frowned and called him Mr
Because in sport he kr
   And so in spite
   That very night
This Mr kr sr

Anon.

Aah!

A Rhyming Quiz

(The answer completes the line. The first two answers are provided, to show you how it works.)

1. One plus three, then halve the answer.   *Two.*
An Australian mammal.   *Kangaroo.*
The stuff we use for washing hair.
Makes the grass wet in the morning.

2. Another name for Tottenham Hotspur.
Another word for slights or insults.
Evergreen trees seen at Christmas.
What a cat does when she's happy.

3. Three times three and add one more makes
Bell inside a London clock.
Very small bird found in Britain.
When the prayer is finished, say

4. The place where you reside is called your
The capital of Italy is
A legendary dwarfish creature.
When your hair's untidy use a

5. Two plus seven minus five makes
What snow and ice do when it's warmer.
Nations fighting one another.
Rooks and crows aren't singing birds. They

6. Granite, limestone, slate are kinds of
It keeps your foot warm in the winter.
The capital of Thailand is
A tall flower found in gardens.

7. If your door is locked you'll need a
A kind of ape—a small one.
He flies and buzzes around the flowers.
How many people in a trio?

8. The opposite of enemy is
Repair a thing that's torn or broken.
When your email's ready, click on
This is the last line. We have reached the

Wendy Cope

Teasing Words

What words are teasing,
annoying, displeasing?
What's sure to put you in a stew?
What makes you cross when
your brain's at a loss for
the answer?

Ans: I'm not telling you!

Rachel Rooney

Irate Pirate

How do you mock a pirate?
Take away his pee.
That will make him so irate!
It's easy. Can't you see?

Ian Larmont

A Trip to Morrow

I started on a journey just about a week ago
For the little town of Morrow in the State of Ohio.
I never was a traveller and I really didn't know
That Morrow had been ridiculed a century or so.
To Morrow, to Morrow, I have to go to Morrow,
The ticket collector told me that I have to go
tomorrow.

I went down to the depot for my ticket and applied
For tips regarding Morrow, interviewed the station
guide.
Said I, 'My friend, I want to go to Morrow and return
No later than tomorrow, for I haven't time to burn.'
To Morrow, to Morrow, I have to go to Morrow,
The ticket collector told me that I have to go tomorrow.

Said he to me, 'Now let me see, if I have heard you
   right,
You want to go to Morrow and come back tomorrow
   night,
You should have gone to Morrow yesterday and back
   today,
The train to Morrow left at two to Morrow yesterday.
To Morrow, to Morrow, I have to go to Morrow,
The ticket collector told me that I have to go tomorrow.

For if you started yesterday to Morrow, don't you see
You should have got to Morrow and returned today
   at three.
The train that started yesterday, now understand me
   right,
Today it gets to Morrow and returns tomorrow night.'
To Morrow, to Morrow, I have to go to Morrow,
The ticket collector told me that I have to go tomorrow.

Said I, 'I guess you know it all, but kindly let me say,
How can I go to Morrow if I leave the town today?'
Said he, 'You cannot go to Morrow today I'll have you
   know,
For that train you see just leaving is the only one to
   go. So—'
Tomorrow, tomorrow, I have to go tomorrow,
The train to Morrow just left today, you'll have to go
   tomorrow.

Anon.

Anagraminal Magic

Does a **hornet** sit on a golden **throne**?
Can a **wasp** sting a creature with **paws**?
If it stays in the sun, will an **ant** get a **tan**?
Will a **ram mar** a lamb without cause?

Will a **butterfly flutter by** quickly?
Is a **leaf** a safe place for a **flea**?
Would a **nit** be quite warm in a cold cocoa **tin**?
Would an **ape** like to eat a green **pea**?

Could a **spider** live in **prides** like a lion?
Would a **rat** get stuck fast in hot **tar**?
Does a **bubble seem** likely from two **bumblebees**?
Would an **asp** creep and crawl in a **spa**?

All of these questions are silly.
What a dozy old poet I am!
I'm just playing around with the letters
In search of an odd anagram.

John Kitching

What Am I?

I have soft fur,
but I never purr.

I don't go to the park,
and I never bark.

I've a twitching nose,
little claws on my toes.

My tail is small,
but my ears are tall.

I'm bigger than a mouse,
I don't live in the house.

I live in a hutch.
Now I've told you too much!

I am a . . .

Jo Peters

Red Alert!

I'm a . . .

Sun-dweller
Gas-brother
Fast-burner
Match-lover
Wet-hater
Flame-thrower
Coal-licker
Smoke-blower
Dark-splitter
Hearth-baker
Spark-spitter
Ash-maker
Wax-melter
Wood-torcher
Ice-breaker
Skin-scorcher
Paint-peeler
Hot-header
Fate-sealer
Quick-spreader

What am I?

Graham Denton

Real Problems

1.
If a supermarket trolley weighs 5 kilos and
the baby, standing inside it, weighs
12 kilos and his father
puts 6 tins of tomatoes
each weighing 400 grams
into the trolley . . . work out

a)   how far the trolley will move before
        the baby drops a tin over the side;
        and
b)   if adding a packet of biscuits
        will make for more or less trouble.

2.
If I have an apple costing 10p
and you have a packet of crisps that costs 20p,
and I give you
three bites of the apple
(but the third bite has a brown bit),
and you give me
twelve crisps
(of which two are tiny and one
is burnt and sour);
do we both feel satisfied
or somehow cheated?

Dave Calder

Eh?

WHAT?

Runs All Day

Runs all day but never walks,
Often murmurs, never talks.
It has a bed, but never sleeps.
It has a mouth, but never eats.

Anon.

White Sheep

White sheep, white sheep, on a blue hill,
When the wind stops, you all stand still.
When the wind blows, you walk away slow.
White sheep, white sheep, where do you go?

Christina Rossetti

The Little Gentleman

There is a little gentleman
That wears the yellow trews,
A dirk below his doublet,
For sticking of his foes.

He's in a stinging posture
Where'er you do him see,
And if you offer violence
He'll stab his dirk in thee.

Anon.

Gleaming Silvery Hair

Gleaming silvery hair
streaming down my
bony back;
bones of stony grey
and slimy black.
Always rushing fast
but never moving along
my raging roar
is my long lifegiver's song.

Penny Kent

I Rhyme With . . .

I rhyme with paddock.
My name is in code.
I sound like a place
but I have no road.
I'm often battered
but never beaten.
I have no hands
but my fingers are eaten.

Geraldine Aldridge

Not a Cow

Though not a cow
I have horns;
Though not an ass
I carry a pack-saddle;
And wherever I go
I leave silver behind me.

Anon.

Find the Spoonerisms!

William Archibald Spooner (1844–1930) was Dean of New College, Oxford. He is said to have had the habit of accidentally exchanging the sounds at the beginnings of words, with amusing results. These phrases came to be known as spoonerisms. See if you can work out the real meaning of the ones below.

1) I've toiled and sweated for many an hour;
I'm stopping now to shake a tower.
Then I'll have cocoa in a mug
And fight a liar and be real snug.

2) The teacher complains while
The pupil sits and squirms:
'You have hissed my mystery lessons
And tasted two worms!'

Eric Finney

Do you know the answer?

Nora, Dora, Ritchie, Laura, Mitchie, and Cora

If Nora and Dora are richer than Ritchie
But Ritchie and Dora are poorer than Laura
And Ritchie's a titchy bit richer than Mitchie
But Mitchie and Nora are richer than Cora
And Nora's more riches make Ritchie feel twitchy,
Then which is the richer and which is the poorer?

David Bateman

Have you worked it out?

Code Shoulder

'L.O.' Z. I.
'L.O.' Z. U.
'R. U. O.K?' I. Z.
'I. B. O.K,' U. Z.
'I. 1. 2. C. U.' Z. I.
'Y?' Z. U.
'U. R. D. 1. 4. I.' I. Z.
'O. I!' U. Z.
'U. R. A. D.R.' Z. I.
'O!' Z. U.
'I. B. D. 1. 4. U. 2.' I. Z.
'N.E. I.D.R. Y?' U. Z.
'I. B. A. B.U.T. 4. N.E.1. 2. C.' Z. I.
'I. 8. U.' Z. U.
'O. D.R!' Z. I.

Barrie Wade

Roomers

'A view herd thin ewes?'
'There shore summit zap end.'
'Wear zit go win gone?'
'Watt sit taller bout?'
'Wide know once top it?'
'Aye mutter lid is custard.'
'Meat who toe telly discus dead.'
'Sum won or tabby maid toot ache theory sponsor
   billy tea.'
'Two write ice head eggs act lea this aim.'
'That rubble width hems the rawl tour can know
   whack shun.'
'Press icily eye cud hunters edit bet term mice elf.'

Nick Toczek

Algie's Trick

My friend Algie told me to think of a number,
So I thought of three,
(Useful for triangles
And three-legged stools).

'Double it,' he said,
So I doubled it. Two threes are . . .
Six,
(What the egg man calls half a dozen).

'Add on four,' my friend said,
So I added four. Six and four are . . .
Ten,
(Just handy for my fingers).

'Halve it,' said Algie,
So I took away one hand.
Half of ten is . . .
Five.

'And now take away the number you first thought of,'
he said,
So I took three away from five . . .
'And the answer is two!' he said.

'Brilliant!' I said. 'How did you know that?'
'It always is,' said Algie.
'But supposing I'd chosen five?' I said.
'Still two,' said Algie.

So I tried it.
Five doubled is ten . . .
Add on four is fourteen . . .
Halve it, is seven . . .
And take away the number you first thought of . . .
Two again!

Then I tried it with thirty-seven thousand,
Eight hundred and forty-two and a half.
It took ages !
And would you believe it?!?!
The answer was two!

And when I tried it on Grandad,
The answer was still two.
'What number did you choose, Grampa?' I asked.
'I never chose a number,' he said, 'I chose a letter.'
'What do you mean?'
'I chose X.'
'X?'
'Yes.'
'What do you mean?'

'Well,' he said, 'X . . .
Double it, you've got two Xes . . .
Add on four, you've got two Xes and four . . .
Halve it, you've got one X and two . . .
Take away the X and you've got . . .'
'TWO!' I shouted.

It made me think.

Gerard Benson

W

The King sent for his wise men all
    To find a rhyme for W;
When they had thought a good long time
But could not think of a single rhyme,
    'I'm sorry,' said he, 'to trouble you.'

James Reeves

Orange Silver Sausage

Some words I've studied for a time,
Like orange, silver, sausage;
But as for finding them a rhyme,
I'm at a total lossage.

Colin West

Whodunnit

Last night there was a murder.
Earl Acrostic had been shot.
Nobody knows who did it,
The police no clues have got.

Hundreds of constables have searched all the house.
Every man there did his best.
But who had done this ghastly deed?
Until the killer was caught who could rest?

The butler, Len, was an obvious choice,
Lord James and the Countess were too.
Eventually the police had to admit they were stumped.
Reader, do *you* have a clue?

Rob Falconer

back 2 44 bc

Use Julius Caesar's code. Take the coded letter and move two letters further on into the alphabet (i.e. A=C, Z=B).

HSJGSQ AYCQYP KYBC RFGQ AMBC
FC RFMSEFR GR UYQ HSQR EPCYR
FGQ CLCKGCQ UCPC LMR GKNPCQQCB
YLB QRYZZCB FGK GL RFC QCLYRC

Codes can conceal but I'm afraid
they're not much help against a blade

Dave Calder

Times Nine

Nine's a magic number.
Try it and you'll see.
Three you know is powerful
And nine is three times three.

Then take any number,
Multiply by nine,
Split the answer, add the digits,
You'll get nine each time.

Patricia Leighton

Rhyming slang

In rhyming slang, 'apples and pears' means 'stairs' and 'plates of meat' means 'feet'. Each of the following rhymes contains examples of rhyming slang printed in bold. See if you can make sense of them!

Had I enough **bees and honey**?
I felt in my **sky rocket** to see.
Yes, I'm in luck, there's just enough
For a nice cup of **Rosy Lee**.

Round the **Johnny Horner**
And up the **frog and toad**,
Wearing my brand new **daisy roots**
On my two **fried eggs** I strode.

Wearing my fashionable **whistle and flute**,
With a **tit for tat** on my head.
Waving goodbye to my **trouble and strife**,
In my **jam jar** off I sped.

As my usual **Sydney Harbour**
Ran a comb through my **Barnet Fair**,
He said, 'Would you **Adam and Eve** it:
You've got a big bald spot there.'

'When you brush your **Hampstead Heath**,'
Said the dentist, 'Are you using fluoride?'
I couldn't say a **dicky bird**
With my **north and south** open wide.

Eric Finney

2 Ys

2 ys u r
2 ys u b
I c u r
2 ys 4 me.

Anon.

Eh?

The Sleeping Bag

Written for The South Polar Times *in 1911*

On the outside grows the furside, on the inside grows
the skinside.
So the furside is the outside, and the skinside is in
the inside.
As the skinside is the inside, and the furside is the
outside;
One 'side' likes the skinside inside, and the furside
on the outside.
Others like the skinside outside, and the furside on
the inside;
As the skinside is the hardside, and the furside is the
soft side.
If you turn the skinside outside, thinking you will
side with that 'side',
Then the soft side, furside's inside, which some argue
is the wrong side.
If you turn the furside outside, as you say it grows on
that side;
Then your outside's next the skinside, which for
comfort's not the right side:
For the skinside is the cold side, and your outside's
not your warm side;
And two cold sides coming side by side are not right
sides one 'side' decides.
If you decide to side with that 'side', turn the
outside, furside, inside:
Then the hard side, cold side, skinside's beyond all
question, inside outside.

Herbert George Ponting

My First Is In . . .

My first is in crystals but not in float.
My second's in dazzling but not in coat.
My third is in soft and in frostbite.
My fourth is in winter and swirling and white.
My whole is a blanket that's freezing at night.

Penny Kent

What Book Am I?

Turn my pages, reader.
I am no ordinary book,
I am not a storyteller,
yet worth your long hard look.

An armchair traveller
can climb mountains, swim my seas,
marvel at the range I cover,
visit many countries.

I am well named after
a giant who shouldered the Earth.
Geography holds no terror;
in me it takes its birth.

Debjani Chatterjee

Have you worked it out?

A Riddle

We are little airy creatures,
All of different voice and features;
One of us in glass is set,
One of us you'll find in jet.
T'other you may see in tin,
And the fourth a box within.
If the fifth you should pursue,
It can never fly from you.

Jonathan Swift

Where in the World?

Where in the world does tomorrow
come before yesterday?
Where does the past follow future
and August come before May?

And where on earth would you find
a cart in front of a horse,
and where does three come way after four
while fifth comes just before fourth?

Trevor Parsons

Our Joe

Our Joe wants to know
if your Joe will lend our Joe your Joe's banjo.
If your Joe won't lend our Joe
your Joe's banjo,
our Joe won't lend your Joe
our Joe's banjo
when our Joe has a banjo!

Anon.

Hee-hee!

Codswallop!

Betcha can't say this one . . .

The swish Swiss fresh fish shop serves such lush fish
   teas.
Each fish dish a wish list, fresh flesh from Swiss seas.
Fat Flat Fish, Battered Cat Fish, you can cram Clam
   Pan Fries,
The swell shell smells sell well, grab a fab Crab Dab
   Pie.
Sip a Squid Squash, nibble posh nosh, try a
   hotchpotch of chips,
While the crook cook cooks fluke soups with Fish
   Finger dips.

Hey . . .

. . . what codswallop, sham scallop, it's a Swiss fish
   teas tease.
Phoney fish biz, it's a Swiss swiz, cos the Swiss have
   no seas!

Maureen Haselhurst

Aah!

Light as a Feather

Light as a feather,
Nothing in it.
A stout man can't hold it
More than a minute.

Anon.

Some Say I Am Golden

Some say I am golden.
No ear can detect me,
But whisper my name
And I am broken.

Cynthia Rider

The Man Who Made it Did Not Want It

The man who made it
Did not want it.
The man who bought it did not need it.
The man who used it never saw it.
What was it?

Duncan Williamson

Of Course

In olden days there lived a lad
Who got thrown into jail,
And as he didn't fancy it
The lad began to wail.

They slung him in a cold dark cell
With four walls to surround him.
No doors, no windows—just a chair,
But oh, they hadn't bound him.

And so he rubbed his hands together,
Made them **sore** as he could bear,
Then with the **saw** he set to work
And started on the chair.

He soon had sawn it into halves,
And two halves make a **whole**,
So through the **hole** our lad then crawled
Just like a little mole.

And once outside he yelled and yelled
And made himself quite **hoarse**,
Then he jumped on the **horse** and rode away
And escaped from jail—of course!

Clive Webster

The Agranam Nomster

Shlow at the noom
Kuscs yoru blood with a plurs
Raros in the drak

Norstem Argaman
The agranam nomster rrrrrrg
Nemorst Nargama

Paul Cookson

Pardon?

Turn this contradictory poem into one that makes sense—and scans better—by adding the prefix 'dis' to six of its words as you read it aloud.

I don't like you—
In fact I think you're nice.
I don't trust you—
I count on your advice.
I'd never obey you
Go on . . . give me a task!
Nor would I please you—
I'm here to help . . . just ask!
I'd never regard you,
Although I might pretend;
Nor would I miss you—
Why would I?—you're my friend!

Philip Waddell

shhh . . .

My first is in shhh . . .
But never in CLANG!
My second's in listen
But never in sang
My third is in lullaby
But isn't in song
My fourth is in echo
Long after it's gone
My fifth can be found
In knock, know, and knee
My sixth isn't found (or is it?)
In the sound of the sea
My last letter's easy.
Are you anywhere near?
For you'll only hear me
When there's nothing to hear.

Roger Stevens

WHAT IS IT?

56

Three Anagriddles

This system gets the message through:
Here come dots—and dashes too.
(Three words: 3, 5, 4)

I'm a dot in place
And my piece of the action
Is to separate
The whole from the fraction.
(Three words: 1, 7, 5)

On an island
In New York Bay:
Built to stay free
In the USA.

(Three words: 6, 2, 7)

Eric Finney

What Am I?

Now here's a little riddle:
What am I, do you think?
I bang nails into woodwork with my head.

No you're wrong!
I'm not a hammer.
I'm a very stupid fellow with a headache
and I think I'll go to bed.

Barry Buckingham

Ummm?

Noel
(a Christmas poem)

Clue: read it aloud.

a b c d e f g h
i j k m n o p q
r s t u v w x y z

Anne Greer

Round the Rugged Rock

Round and round the rugged rock
The ragged rascal ran,
How many Rs are there in that?
Now tell me if you can.

Anon.

I'm soaking wet yet always dry.
I live nine times but never die.
What am I?
When I go flying underground,
I'm always seen but never found.
What am I?

I'm in the dark behind the star.
I'm on the wheels beneath the car.
What am I?
I'm in the cup behind the dish.
I'm on the chips beneath the fish.
What am I?

David Bateman

Acknowledgements

Every effort has been made to trace and contact copyright holders before publication and we are grateful to all those who have granted us permission. We apologize for any inadvertent errors and will be pleased to rectify these at the earliest opportunity.

Geraldine Aldridge: 'I Rhyme With . . .' copyright © Geraldine Aldridge.
David Bateman: 'Nora, Dora, Ritchie, Laura, Mitchie and Cora' and 'Q' copyright © David Bateman.
Gerard Benson: 'Algie's Trick' copyright © Gerard Benson.
Barry Buckingham: 'What Am I?' copyright © Barry Buckingham.
Dave Calder: 'Real Problems' and 'back 2 44 bc' copyright © Dave Calder.
Richard Caley: 'Fighting Men' copyright © Richard Caley.
James Carter: 'Found It YET?' copyright © James Carter.
Debjani Chatterjee: 'What Book Am I?' copyright © Debjani Chatterjee.
Paul Cookson: 'The Agranam Nomster' copyright © Paul Cookson.
Wendy Cope: 'A Rhyming Quiz' copyright © Wendy Cope.
Graham Denton: 'Red Alert!' copyright © Graham Denton.
Rob Falconer: 'Growing Up in Rome' and 'Whodunnit' copyright © Rob Falconer.
Eric Finney: 'Peggy Babcock', 'Find the Spoonerisms!', 'Rhyming Slang' and 'Three Anagriddles' copyright © Eric Finney.
Anne Greer: 'Noel' copyright © Anne Greer.
Maureen Haselhurst: 'Codswallop!' copyright © Maureen Haselhurst.
Beverley Johnson: 'Four Sports' copyright © Beverley Johnson.
Penny Kent: 'Gleaming Silvery Hair' and 'My First Is In . . .' copyright © Penny Kent.
Daphne Kitching: 'IT ('s) a Riddle' copyright © Daphne Kitching.
John Kitching: 'Anagraminal Magic' copyright © John Kitching.
Ian Larmont: 'Irate Pirate' copyright © Ian Larmont.
Patricia Leighton: 'Times Nine' copyright © Patricia Leighton.
Trevor Millum: 'That Dreadful Pupil from Leicester' copyright © Trevor Millum.
Trevor Parsons: 'Where in the World?' copyright © Trevor Parsons.
Jo Peters: 'What Am I?' copyright © Jo Peters.
James Reeves: 'W' © James Reeves from *Complete Poems for Children* (Heinemann). Reprinted by permission of the James Reeves Estate.
Cynthia Rider: 'Some Say I Am Golden' copyright © Cynthia Rider.
Rachel Rooney: 'Teasing Words' copyright © Rachel Rooney.

Answers

p. 8 **Found it Yet?**: love
p. 9 **IT ('s) a Riddle**: computer
p. 10 **Growing Up in Rome**:
Roman numerals: 4 = IV; 6 = VI; 40 = XL; 54 = LIV; 99 = IC ('icy')
p. 11 **Fighting Men**: gladiators
p. 12 **Four Sports**:
1) I serve an ace / Forehand return / Cross-court volley / Just tap it
over the net
(Answer: Tennis)
2) I kick the ball / To score a goal / A well-placed header / Can please
the crowd
(Answer: Football)
3) I dive off the springboard / And land in the pool / Small kids do
doggy paddle / I prefer the crawl
(Answer: Swimming)

4) The ball's an odd shape / We group in a scrum / I score a try /
Then convert and we've won
(Answer: Rugby)

p. 14 That Dreadful Pupil from Leicester:
There was a young pupil from Leicester / Who would go to her
teachers and pester / She would lock them indoors / Glue their feet to
the floors / Till finally they came to arrest her

p. 15 Ounce Poem:
A girl who weighed many on ounce, / Used language I dare not
pronounce, / For a fellow unkind / Pulled her chair out behind / Just
to see (so he said) if she'd bounce.

p. 15 She Called Him Mr:
She frowned and called him Mr / Because in sport he kissed her / And
so in spite / That very night / This Mister kissed her sister

p. 16 A Rhyming Quiz:
1) two, kangaroo, shampoo, dew; 2) Spurs, slurs, firs, purrs; 3) ten, Big
Ben, wren, Amen; 4) home, Rome, gnome, comb; 5) four, thaw, war,
caw; 6) rock, sock, Bangkok, hollyhock; 7) key, chimpanzee, bee, three;
8) friend, mend, send, end

p. 24 **What Am I?** : rabbit

p. 25 **Red Alert!** : fire

p. 27 **Runs All Day**: river

p. 27 **White Sheep**: clouds

p. 27 **The Little Gentleman**: bee

p. 28 **Gleaming Silvery Hair**: waterfall

p. 28 **I Rhyme With . . .** : fish

p. 29 **Not a Cow**: snail

p. 30 Find the Spoonerisms! :
1) I'm stopping now to take a shower; And light a fire and be real snug.
2) 'You have missed my history lessons / And wasted two terms!'

p. 31 Nora, Dora, Ritchie, Laura, Mitchie, and Cora:
There are three possible answers: 1) Nora is richest, followed by Laura,
Dora, Ritchie, Mitchie, and finally Cora
or 2) Laura is richest, followed by Dora, Nora, Ritchie, Mitchie and Cora
or 3) Laura is richest, followed by Nora, Dora, Ritchie, Mitchie and
Cora.

p. 32 Code Shoulder:
'Hello,' said I. / 'Hello,' said you. / 'Are you OK?' I said. / 'I be OK,' you
said. / 'I want to see you,' said I. / 'Why?' said you. / 'You are de one
for I,' I said. / 'Oh I!' you said. / 'You are a dear,' said I. / 'Oh!' said you.
/ 'I be de one for you too,' I said. / 'Any idea why?' you said. / 'I be a
beauty for anyone to see,' said I. / 'I hate you,' said you. / 'Oh dear!'
said I.

p. 33 **Roomers / Rumours**:
'Have you heard the news?' / 'They're sure summat's happened.' /
'Where's it going on?' / 'What's it all about?' / 'Why'd no one stop it?' /
'I'm utterly disgusted.' / 'Me too, totally disgusted.' / 'Someone ought
to be made to take the responsibility.' / 'Too right. I said exactly the
same.' / 'The trouble with them's they're all talk and no action.' /
'Precisely. I couldn't have said it better myself.'

p. 38 **Whodunnit**: Len the butler (acrostic)

p. 40 **back 2 44 bc**:
Julius Caesar made this code / He thought it was just great / His
enemies were not impressed / And stabbed him in the Senate.

p. 42 **Rhyming Slang**:
Money / pocket / tea; corner / road / boots / legs; suit / hat / wife /
car; barber / hair / believe; teeth / word / mouth.

p. 43 **2 Ys**: Too wise you are / too wise you be / I see you are / too wise
for me.

p. 45 **My First Is In . . .** : snow

p. 46 **What Book Am I?** : atlas

p. 46 **A Riddle**: vowels

p. 47 **Where in the World?** : in a dictionary

p. 50 **Light as a Feather**: breath

p. 51 **Some Say I Am Golden**: silence

p. 51 **The Man Who Made It Did Not Want It**: coffin

p. 54 **The Agranam Nomster / The Anagram Monster**:
Howls at the moon / Sucks your blood with a slurp / Roars in the dark
Monster anagram / The anagram monster grrrrrr /Monster anagram

p. 55 **Pardon?** :
The six words to be prefixed with *dis* are like (line 1), trust (in line 3),
obey (in line 5), please (in line 7), regard (in line 9) and miss (in line
11).

p. 56 **Shhh . . .** : silence

p. 57 **Three Anagriddles**: 1) the Morse Code; 2) a decimal point;
3) Statue of Liberty

p. 60 **Noel**: there is no 'l' in the alphabet listed – 'Noel'.

p. 61 **Round the Rugged Rock**: none. There are no Rs in 'that'.

p. 62 **Q**: talking complete nonsense!